Publisher: Travis Rigby

Author: Julia Marie Schmitt AIFD, CFD, EMC, ICPF, PFCI

Editor: Robin Avni

Art Director: Kathleen Dillinger

Flowers to Wear: The Fascination of Floral Couture was produced by WildFlower Media, Inc.

Ft. Lauderdale, Florida
floristsreview.com

Printed in China

ISBN: 978-1-7337826-7-8

Wildflower.Media

(FRONT COVER)
DESIGNER Tobey Nelson, **PHOTOGRAPHY** Shannon Beauclair, Beauclair Photography

(BACK COVER, CLOCKWISE)
DESIGNER Marie Pauly, **PHOTOGRAPHY** Missy Donovan Photography
DESIGNER Julia Griffin, **PHOTOGRAPHY** Holden Photo
DESIGNER Orit Hertz, **PHOTOGRAPHY** Ilanit Turgeman

The Fascination of Floral Couture

FLOWERS TO WEAR

CURATED BY JULIA MARIE SCHMITT
AIFD, CFD, ICPF, EMC, PFCI

CONTENTS

DESIGNER Courtney Kroymann
PHOTOGRAPHER Beth Joy Photography

DESIGNER COUTURE AND SCARF Carol Jillian
DESIGNER FLORAL ACCESSORIES AND HEADPIECE Françoise Weeks
ART DIRECTION, PHOTOGRAPHY AND STYLING Obsidian + BlushFloral

PREFACE

Discovery from Deconstruction

Botanical couture has been popular for quite a while in Europe. I have so often been inspired by the beauty that so many of those brilliant designers created. At the same time the question kept coming up for me: What are the mechanics behind this? So, about twelve years ago, my own curiosity and perseverance led me to explore this imaginative world.

Through endless trial and error, I worked hard to figure out the form-fitting mechanics along with the materials that were best suited to create the bases for jewelry, head pieces, purses, dresses and other accessories. Deconstructing the flowers and textures allowed me to explore so many new possibilities and designs. As I love delicate details so much, I found that rings, earrings and necklaces were the perfect platforms to create with my snippets of flowers and plants.

Considering that I never had paid much attention to fashion, it is a bit humorous that as the years went by, I became so passionate about designing botanical wearables.

But now, I am no longer alone in my fascination. Botanical couture has gained in popularity as evidenced by the extraordinary work showcased in this book. They, too, have found that floral couture offers one an interesting journey with endless potential.

Françoise Weeks

Owner of Françoise Weeks Florist, Portland, Oregon

INTRODUCTION

FLOWERS TO WEAR: The Fascination of Floral Couture

When I was a little girl, fashion designing was my life! My dolls and my bedroom "design workspace" looked like a scene from *Project Runway*. I spent every free moment sewing original Barbie® couture creations made from scraps of toilet paper, cardboard, Grandma's quilt remnants, seeds and sometimes mud or clay. My school notebooks were filled with evening gown sketches and my shopping trips to Kmart® were spent in the Barbie doll accessory aisle dreaming of the day I could afford a 30-pack of Barbie shoes!

Even though I left my dreams of being a Paris fashion designer behind, I quietly held on to the idea of someday, somehow, being part of the design world. Many years later, when I entered the floral industry, I quickly observed that many of my fellow floral artists where still "playing with dolls". Only these floral couture designers had exchanged their Barbie muses for real models using a new "fabric" made of botanical materials.

Today, designers are still tailoring foliage and incorporating sewing techniques to create form-fitting, exquisite evening dresses. They are experimenting with combining diverse mechanics and techniques to create over-the-top, high-fashion head pieces. They use natural woods in a unique way to design wearable jewelry! In short, floral designers have given themselves permission to "play" with flowers and, in turn, produce gorgeous floral fashion that rival the design houses of Paris, New York and Milan.

Why, you might ask, do floral artists embrace this area of expertise within the industry? The overwhelming response to this question is simple: Because they love it! The designers who grace the pages of this book have found their niche, their happy place that allows them to express themselves as the fashion designers they had secretly kept locked away. They willingly, and exuberantly, give you private access to their floral couture visions and designs.

This "All Access Pass" allows you to window shop, stroll and live vicariously through their inspiring creations. These pages are filled with incredibly beautiful and expressive headpieces, accessories, dresses and whimsical floral ensembles – all created by these passionate floral artists.

You have our permission to "virtually" try on the fashion and prance in the mirror imagining you are wearing these one-of-a-kind fashion creations. A few of the designers have graciously shared their secrets giving you the keys to becoming a Floral Fashionista with step-by-step designs for making floral dresses, floral jewelry, floral halos and more!

We hope you enjoy the fashion salon experience of *Flowers to Wear* and let it inspire your inner fashionista, unlock that floral couture spirit and create to your heart's desire.

May your dreams become a reality and walk down the catwalk!

Julia Marie Schmitt
AIFD, CFD, EMC, ICPF, PFCI

DESIGNER COUTURE AND SCARF Carol Jillian
DESIGNER FLORAL ACCESSORIES AND HEADPIECE Françoise Weeks
ART DIRECTION, PHOTOGRAPHY AND STYLING Obsidian + BlushFloral

ENSEMBLES

ENSEMBLES

DESIGNER Debbie Smyl
PHOTOGRAPHER Caitlyn Blake

Diana Vreeland

"Fashion is part of the daily air and it changes all the time, with all the events. You can even see the approaching of a revolution in clothes. You can see and feel everything in clothes."

DESIGNER Julia Rose
PHOTOGRAPHER Hossay

ENSEMBLES

DESIGNER Julia Rose
PHOTOGRAPHER Cloud Catcher Studio

DESIGNER Orit Hertz
PHOTOGRAPHER Meital Solomon

(Right)
DESIGNER Orit Hertz
PHOTOGRAPHER Ilanit Turgeman

DESIGNER Carol Jillian
PHOTOGRAPHER Felicia Reed Photography

Edith Head

"You can have anything you want in life if you dress for it."

DESIGNER Carol Jillian
PHOTOGRAPHER Tony Redmer

Design by **Loann Burke**
Photography by **Jennifer Gilman, Mark Garber Photography**

Who says that a prom dress or a senior picture can't be floral couture? By creating a once in a lifetime work of wearable art, your daughter or client can make a statement for the big day.

DESIGNER Loann Burke
PHOTOGRAPHER Jennifer Gilman, photographer at Mark Garber Photography

1

Using a full skirt pattern, cut the red felt and sew the pieces together according to the pattern. When using felt, make sure to reinforce the waistband to prevent stretching; also sew in a stiffer fabric at the waist. Use velcro for the closure.

2

Deconstruct the Freedom roses. Apply the petals to the hem line of skirt using a floral adhesive. Felt is an excellent medium for glue to adhere.

3

Attach rose heads onto the skirt creating a pattern.

4

Alternate gluing petals and rose heads in a desire pattern until fabric is completely covered.

5

Take the bodice being worn by your model, glue the petals and roses heads to the bodice in a desired pattern. Then, liberally spray the completed dress with floral preservative.

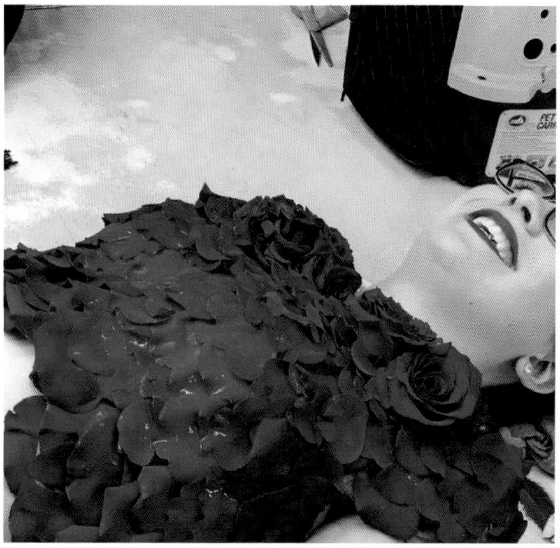

STEP-BY-STEP / *Rose Prom Dress*

BOTANICAL MATERIALS

Freedom roses

MATERIALS

Floral adhesive

Red felt

Stretch bodice

Floral preservative

JE
W

JEWELRY

BRACELETS

(Top)
DESIGNER Tobey Nelson
PHOTOGRAPHER Emily Wandres

(Bottom)
DESIGNER Małgorzata Pawłowska
PHOTOGRAPHER Małgorzata Pawłowska

(Left)
DESIGNER Orit Hertz
PHOTOGRAPHER Shay Kedem Photography

(Top left) **DESIGNER** Denise Kelly, **PHOTOGRAPHER** Cynthia Bennet Photography

(Bottom left) **DESIGNER** Laura Draghici, **PHOTOGRAPHER** Marius Petre Photography

DESIGNER Tobey Nelson
PHOTOGRAPHER Shannon Beauclair, Beauclair Photography

DESIGNER Tuba Oskan
PHOTOGRAPHER Irem Tanman

STEP-BY-STEP / *Stacking Floral Bracelets*

Design by **Susanne Law**
Photography by **Richard Law**

Using fresh plant materials to create the floral bracelets is a wonderful eco-friendly and sustainable option; plants offer a beautiful range of colors and textures. By creating multiple strands of botanical bracelets with different types of plant materials, you can stack them for a custom contemporary look.

1

Thread two boxwood leaves followed by one *Skimmia* berry onto the coated wire. Repeat this pattern until the desired length of the bracelet is reached. Finish the wire ends by using the needle nose plier to create a small scroll.

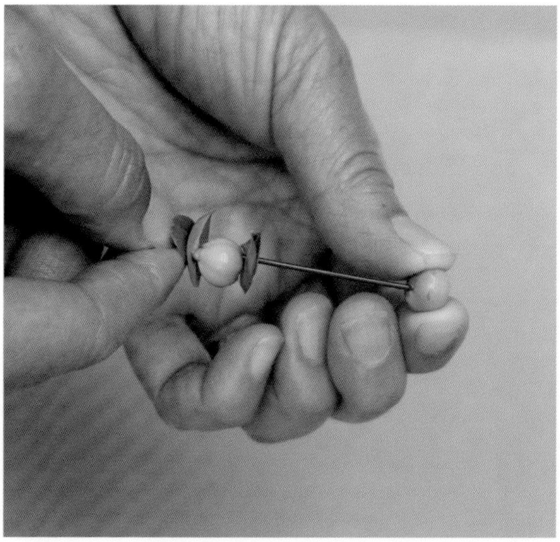

DESIGNER Susanne Law
PHOTOGRAPHER Richard Law

2

Create a second bracelet by threading the Burro's Tail "beads" onto another piece of coated wire. Choose the greener "beads" as they tend to be firmer. To secure the botanicals, use a toothpick to insert floral adhesive between the beads. Do not over glue.

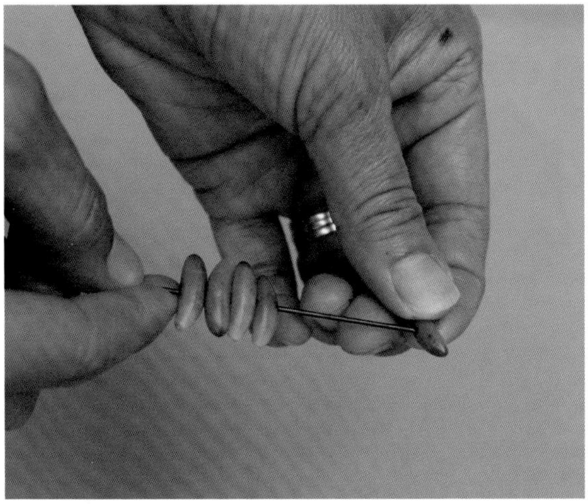

3

Cut a piece of Maiden Hair vine the length that can wrap around the wrist twice. Secure the vine with bullion wire.

4

Add some accents on one of the bracelets by gluing small pieces of Wandering Jew leaves, Burro's Tail bud and *Clematis* floss to the strand.

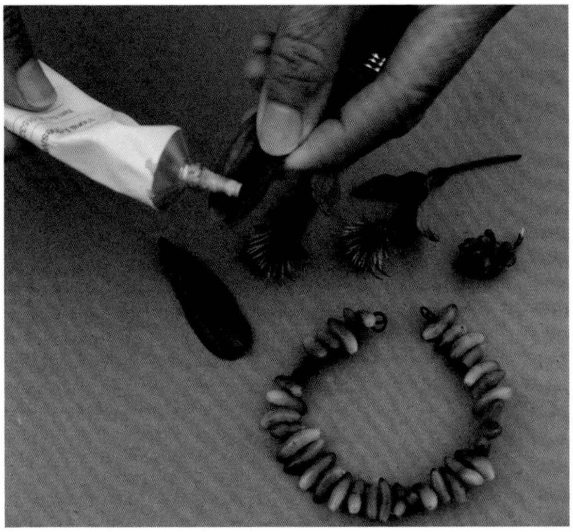

5

Stack the strands creating that perfect botanical bracelet to compliment any fashion attire.

NOTE: *To keep the bracelets fresh for a couple of days, store in an airtight container with a damp paper towel.*

STEP-BY-STEP / *Stacking Floral Bracelets*

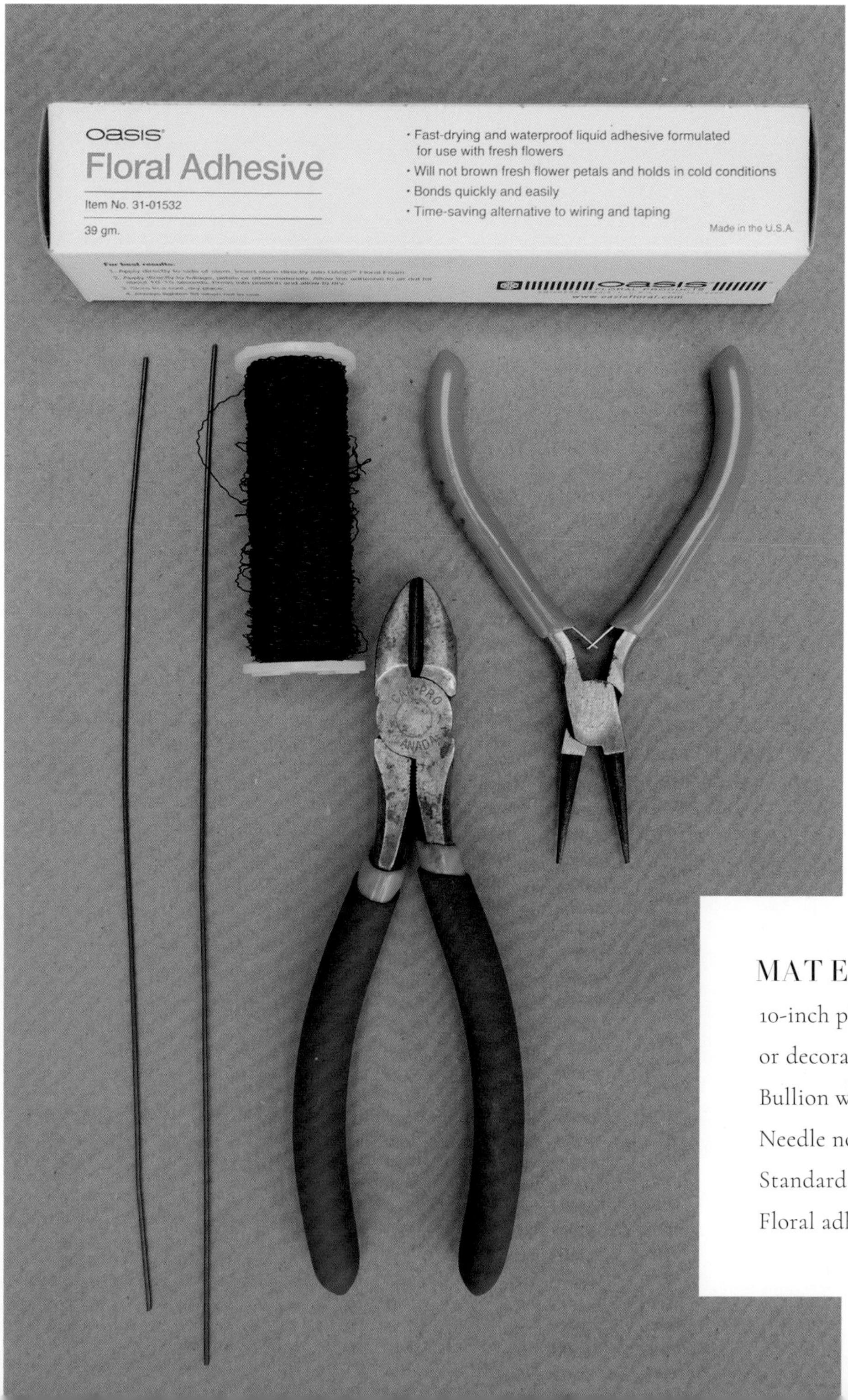

MATERIALS

10-inch piece of No. 18-gauge coated floral wire or decorative floral wire

Bullion wire (dark color)

Needle nose wirecutter

Standard wirecutters

Floral adhesive

BOTANICAL MATERIALS

Green *Skimmia*

Wandering Jew leaves

Burro's tail

Boxwood

Clematis floss

Maiden Hair vine

Kate Spade

"Playing dress-up begins at age five and never truly ends."

NECKLACES

DESIGNER Carol Jillian
PHOTOGRAPHER Jay Barns

DESIGNER Tobey Nelson
PHOTOGRAPHER Shannon Beauclair Photography

DESIGNER Tobey Nelson
PHOTOGRAPHER Suzanne Rothmeyer Photography

JEWELRY / *Necklaces*

(Right)
DESIGNER Kristen Janes
PHOTOGRAPHER Kristin La Voie Photography

(Below)
DESIGNER Tobey Nelson
PHOTOGRAPHER Kim Nowell

DESIGNER Orit Hertz
PHOTOGRAPHER Meital Solomon

DESIGNER Kiki Uyede
PHOTOGRAPHER Simply Sweet Photography

DESIGNER Julia Griffin
PHOTOGRAPHER Holden Photo

DESIGNER Kiki Uyede
PHOTOGRAPHER ellvonie

DESIGNER Rupali Shete Sadalage
PHOTOGRAPHER Erich Schrempp

DESIGNER Donald Yim
PHOTOGRAPHER Alex Choi

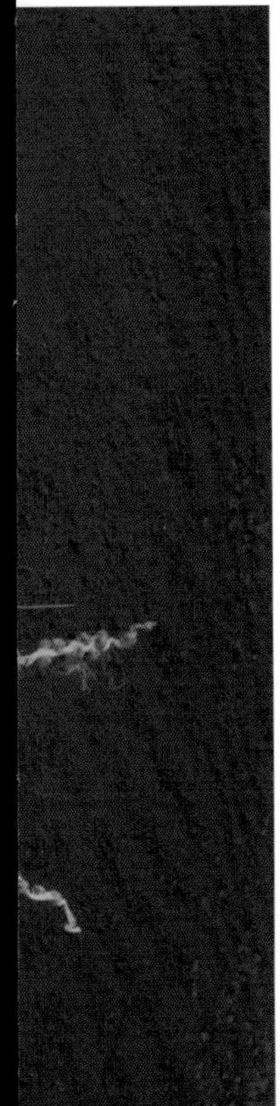

DESIGNER Tuba Oskan
PHOTOGRAPHER Irem Tanman

STEP-BY-STEP | *Bamboo Circle Necklace*

Design by **Lea Romanowski**
Photography by **Fly Free Photography**

You can create a statement piece that can be worn for any occasion. This unique, modern necklace gives the designer the ability to create a form that is reusable. Remove the dried flower and be inspired to create something new. Have fun with it and watch heads turn as you walk into your next event.

1

Cover a 1 to 1½-inch bamboo pole with painter's tape. Using a chop saw, slowly cut half-inch pieces from both ends of the bamboo. This will give you a variation of circle diameters. Choice the pieces you want to use and remove the tape.

2

Using a Dremel and a sanding tool, sand the interior and exterior surfaces of the cut bamboo to remove the splinters; this will also allow the paint to adhere.

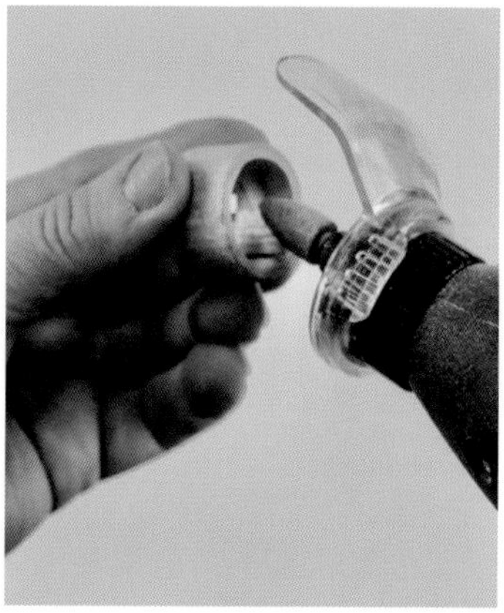

3

Arrange the bamboo pieces creating the desired shape for the necklace. With a felt marker, make a black dot at every point where bamboo edges will touch each other. Keep the pieces in order.

4

Drill a hole the width of your aluminum wire through each black mark, one at a time, placing them back in the order you have created. Thread the aluminum wire though the holes one piece at a time, leaving 1-inch of wire at each end to make the finishing loops.

If you will be creating several layers, thread the main line first then wire the lower pieces up into the main piece.

5

Spray paint the bamboo necklace. Let the necklace dry; then add a second coat. Allow three hours to completely dry.

6

Insert *Craspedia* from the front side of the bamboo. Flip the necklace over and cold glue into place. Repeat with *Celosia*.

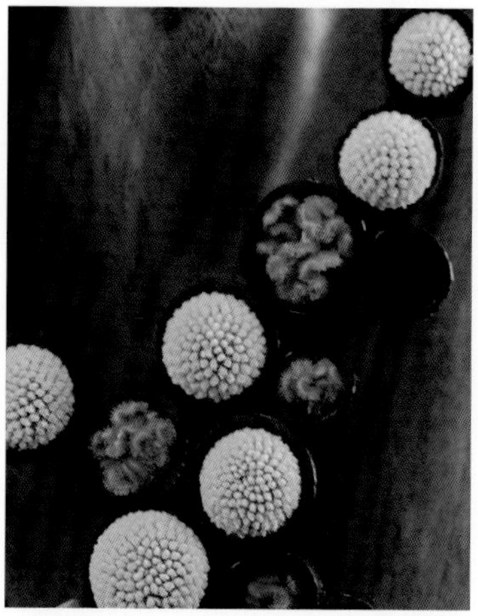

DESIGN: Lea Romanowski
PHOTOGRAPHY: Remember When Photography

7

Create small fabric balls and insert them into a few of the bamboo holes in the front of necklace. Flip over and hot glue into place.

8

Cut felt circles and hot glue to back of each bamboo piece

9

With the necklace facing you, create loops at each end of the aluminum wire with a needle nose pliers. Attach your desired chain to the loops created.

BOTANICAL MATERIALS

Craspedia (Billy Balls)

Celosia

MATERIALS

1 to 1½-inch bamboo pole

Painter's tape

Chop saw

Dremel

Sander

Felt marker

Drill

Black aluminum wire

Black spray paint

Felt

Needle nose pliers

RINGS

John Galliano

"The joy of dressing is an art."

(Left) **DESIGNER** Denise Kelly, **PHOTOGRAPHER** Cynthia Bennett Photography

DESIGNER Laura Draghici, **PHOTOGRAPHER** Marius Petre Photography

DESIGNER Tobey Nelson
PHOTOGRAPHER Suzanne Rothmeyer Photography

DESIGNER Brenda Garcia
PHOTOGRAPHER Brenda Garcia

DESIGNER Courtney Kroymann
PHOTOGRAPHER Beth Joy Photography

JEWELRY

EARRINGS

DESIGNER Anika Wilson
PHOTOGRAPHER Katelyn Mallett Photography

DESIGNER Julia Griffin
PHOTOGRAPHER Holden Photo

Alber Elbaz

“Style is the only thing you can’t buy. It’s not in a shopping bag, a label, or a price tag. It’s something reflected from our soul to the outside world—an emotion.”

DESIGNER Tobey Nelson
PHOTOGRAPHER Suzanne Rothmeyer Photography

(Left)
DESIGNER Betsy Borden
PHOTOGRAPHER Jessie and Dallin Photoography

(Left)
DESIGNER Wendy Evans
PHOTOGRAPHER Brandi McComb Photography

DESIGNER Laura Draghici
PHOTOGRAPHER Marius Petre Photography

STEP-BY-STEP / *Liriope Loop Earrings*

Design by **Susanne Law**
Photography by **Richard Law**

Create an intriguing statement piece for any occasion with minimal plant material. By using some wire and a few stems of foliage, you can create one-of-a-kind *Liriope* loop earring.

1

Starting with the wide end of the blade of grass, tightly roll the entire piece of lily grass.

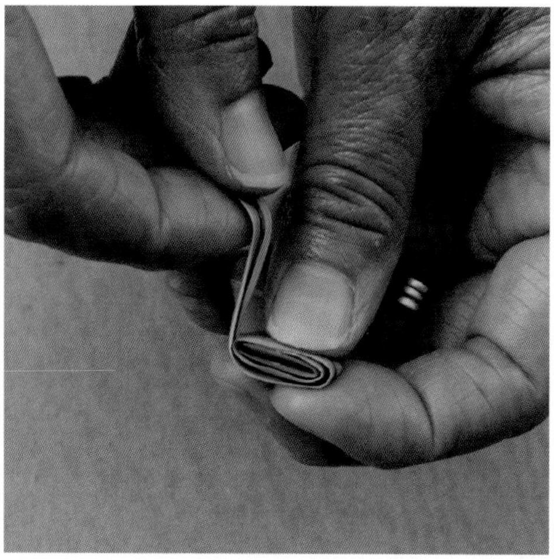

2

Cut the No. 18-gauge wire at a sharp edge creating a needle point. Pierce the botanical roll in the middle with wire. Repeat with each piece of lily grass.

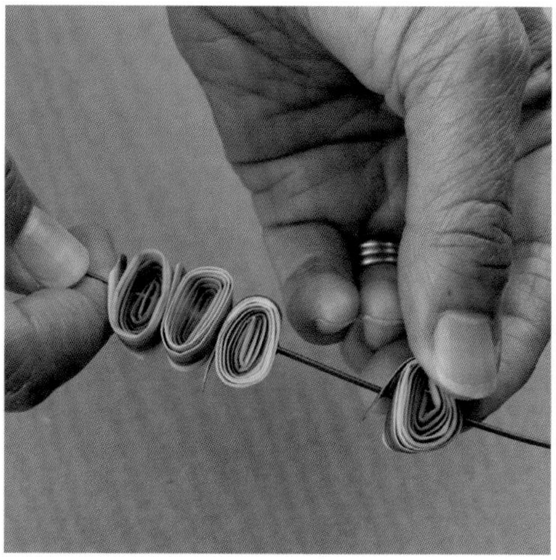

3

Stack the lily grass rolls close to the middle of the wire, leaving 4 inches of wire at the top portion of the rolls and 5 inches of wire on the bottom portion of the rolls. The lily grass rolls will take up approximately 2 inches. Cover the wire by wrapping it with binding wire.

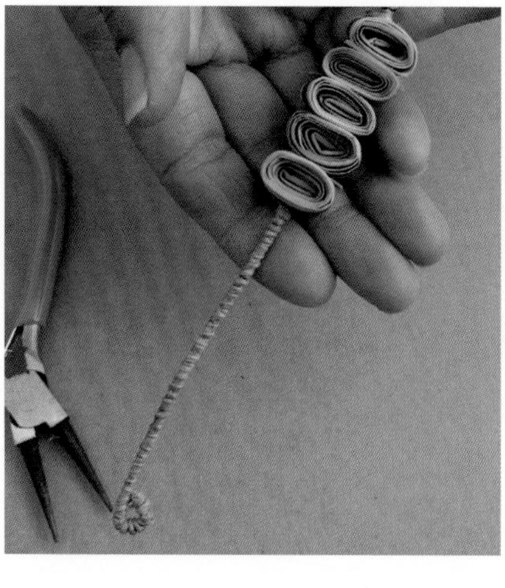

4

Create a scroll pattern on the top and bottom of the lily grass bundles.

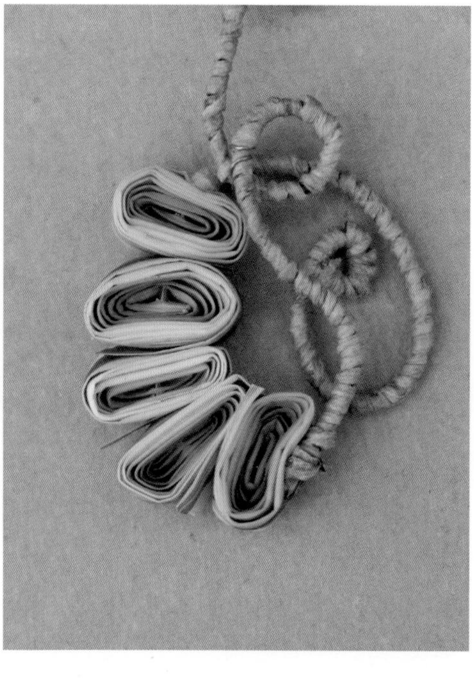

5

Add the O-ring/jump ring and shepherd's hook to the top of the design. Make sure that the shepherd's hook is in the correct position for the earring to hang correctly. Reshape the binding wire construction to desired look.

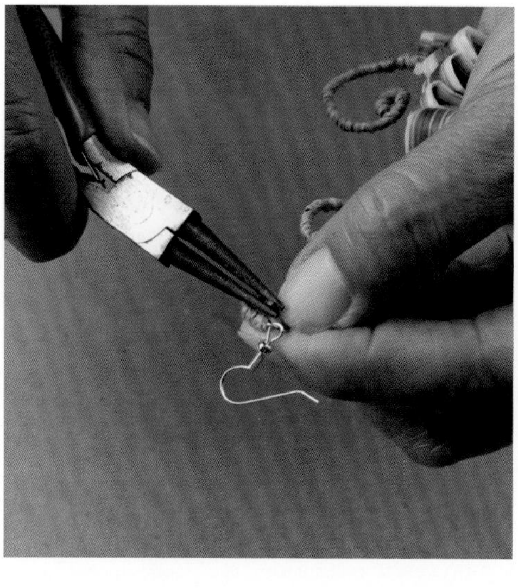

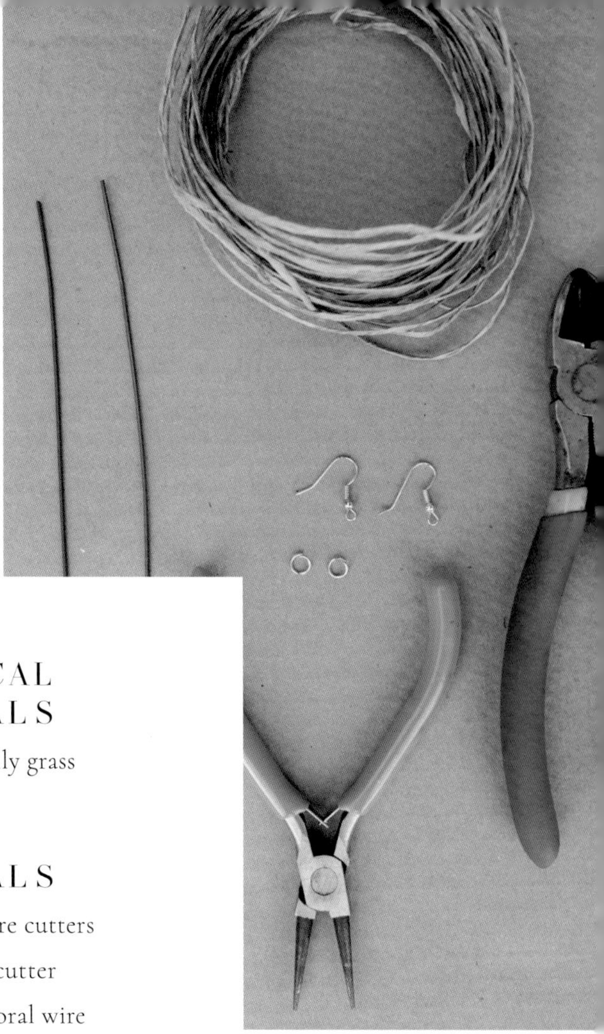

BOTANICAL MATERIALS

Five pieces of lily grass

MATERIALS

Needle nose wire cutters
Standard wire cutter
No. 18-gauge floral wire
(approximately 11 inches)
Binding wire
Shepherd's hook and O-ring

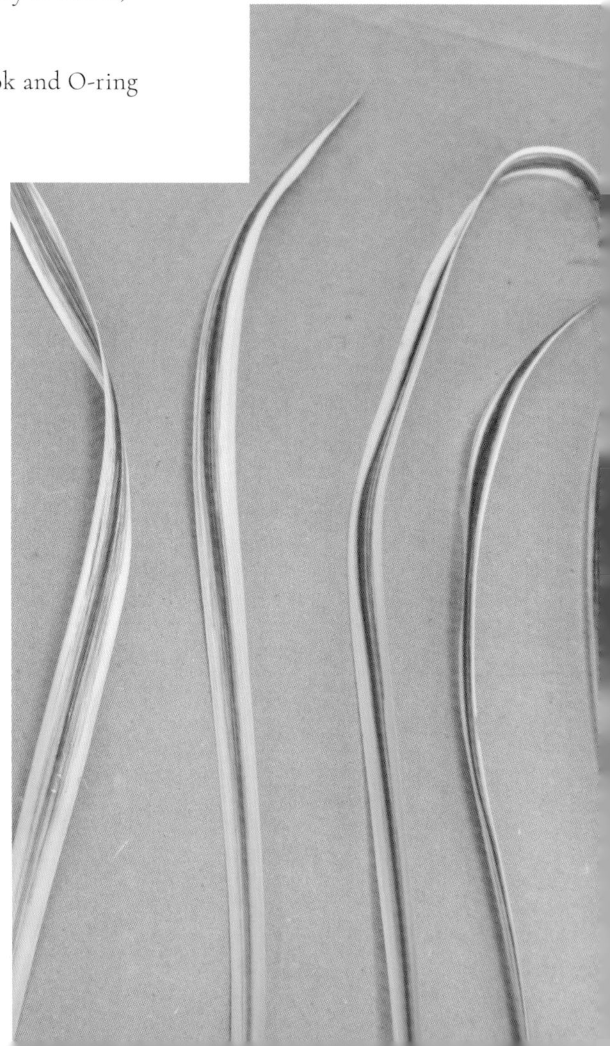

DESIGNER Susanne Law
PHOTOGRAPHER Richard Law

TATTOOS

TATTOOS

TATTOOS

DESIGNER Gina Thresher
PHOTOGRAPHER Rachel Davis

TATTOOS

DESIGNER Coral Shortt
PHOTOGRAPHER Peter Bruyns

DESIGNER Coral Shortt
PHOTOGRAPHER Mint Tea Photography

DESIGNER Annise Lorel
PHOTOGRAPHER Tristen Williams

Rachel Zoe

"Style is a way to say who you are without having to speak."

TATTOOS

DESIGNER Tobey Nelson
PHOTOGRAPHER Jen Lee Light

(Right)
DESIGNER Elli Jespersen
PHOTOGRAPHER Small Flower Floral Studio

(Left)
DESIGNER Tobey Nelson
PHOTOGRAPHER Aly Willis

TATTOOS

DESIGNER Betsy Borden
PHOTOGRAPHER Jessie and Dallian Photography

DESIGNER Laura Draghici
PHOTOGRAPHER Marius Petre Photography

TATTOOS

DESIGNER Julia Griffin
PHOTOGRAPHER Holden Photo

STEP-BY-STEP | *A Floral Tattoo*

Design by **Ania Norwood**
Photography by **Beata Rasmus**

Floral tattoos are a fun and trendy accessory that add an elegant sophistication. They can be created in any shape and size in order to make a personal style statement. These chic flowers to wear can be designed in advance and are easy for any individual to attach by his or herself to any part of the body. Depending on the look and dramatic impact, you can create multiple designs using the same method. Just like normal tattoos, each design can be very different. Have fun creating!

1

Create a template by drawing your desired shape on a piece of paper. Cut out the design. Check the template size against the desired location on the body. Using this pattern, cut out the desired shape from the peel-and-stick felt.

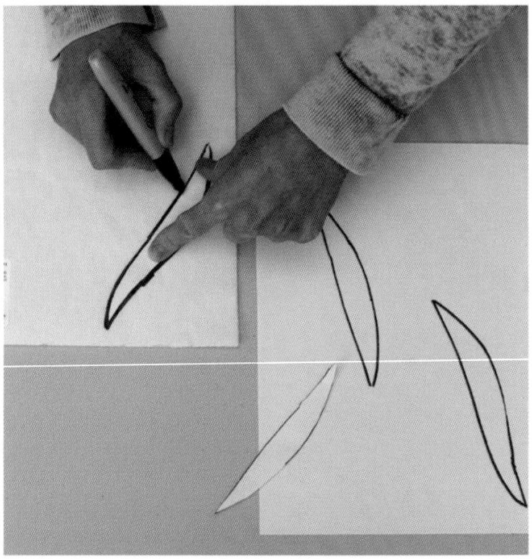

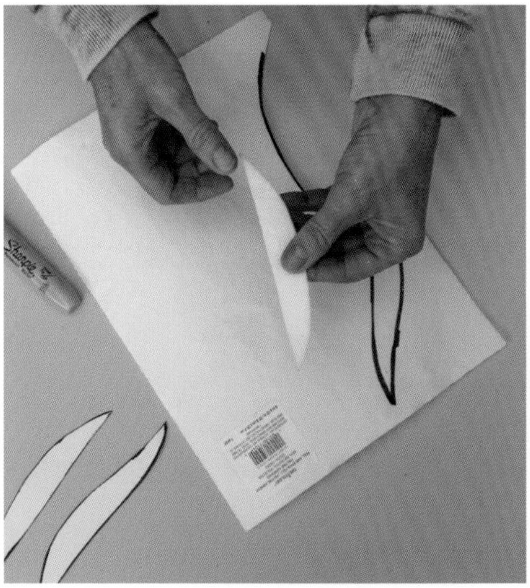

Pro Tip: *Remember that the actual size of the finished design will be bigger than the template.*

2

Adhere a small piece of double-sided tape to the back side of the felt. Attach to a paper tube or bottle. The rounded shape resembles the curve of an arm or leg and will help with covering the felt with botanical materials.

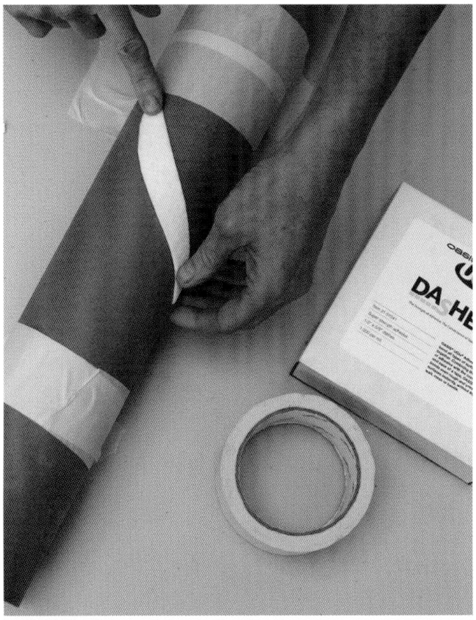

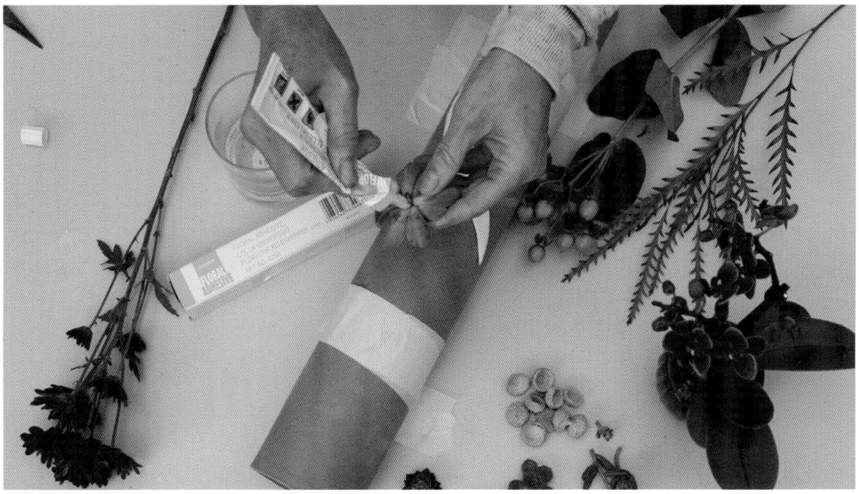

3

Cut the flowers heads flat with no stems. Glue the botanicals starting with the larger varieties, such as succulents, to the felt and then add mums, acorn heads, smaller succulents, etc. Continue to repeat these steps until you have covered the entire surface. The most beautiful and delicate flowers should be glued into place last. Fill any gaps with leaves and *Hypericum* so that no felt is showing.

Pro Tip: *If you have never worked with cold glue before, the trick is to add glue to the product you plan to use as well as the surface you will be attaching it to, and then let it air dry for about 15 seconds before attaching. This will help the product stick better and stay in place. When attaching bigger and heavier product, help them to stay in place by holding gently for a moment. Another good idea is to place the flowers on the felt first without glue, that way you can visualize the design better and make any necessary adjustments before adhering product with glue.*

STEP-BY-STEP / *A Floral Tattoo*

4

Once you are happy with your tattoo design, gently remove it from the paper tube or bottle. DO NOT remove the paper backing from the felt until applying it to the body. Let the glue dry for 30 minutes and then spray with a finishing product and let dry.

5

If your tattoo is being delivered to its recipient, place it in a delivery box and add the following information describing the proper attachment of the tattoo to the body:

In order to attach your tattoo properly to the desired part of the body, first ensure that the body surface is free from any natural or applied moisture by gently wiping the area with a degreaser like tonic or antiseptic alcohol. Do not use antiseptic close to eye area.

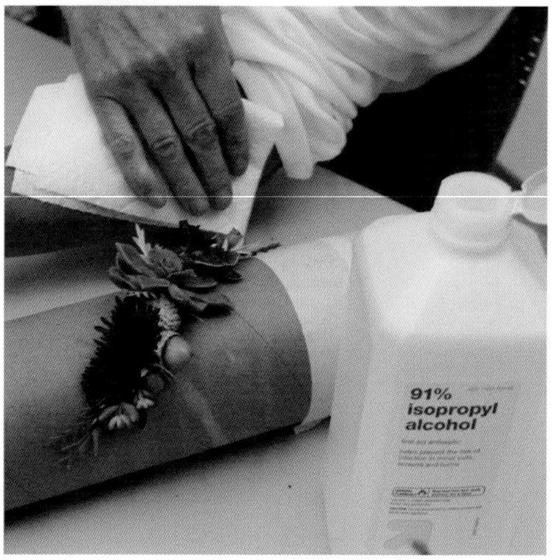

6

When the skin is dry, peel off the paper backing of the felt so the sticky part is revealed. Apply the tattoo to the desired location on the body. Press it gently but firmly, especially the ends, to ensure proper attachments.

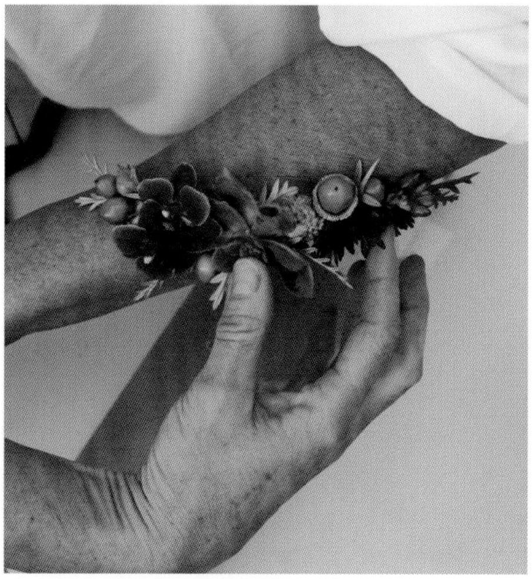

Pro Tip: *Before peeling off the backing, it is highly recommended that you double check the placement of the tattoo. Once you stick it to the skin, removal is not recommended because it might not adhere the second time.*

BOTANICAL MATERIALS

Hypericum

Succulents-small variety of sizes

(*Echeveria, Graptopetalum,*

Sedum etc.)

Mini *Phalaenopsis* orchids

Chrysanthemum tros santini

Bleached acorn heads

Grevillea

MATERIALS

Felt marker

Paper

Scissors

Double-sided tape

Cold adhesive glue

Masking tape

Peel-and-stick felt from a craft store

Cutters or shears

Paper tube or bottle

Floral finishing spray

HAI

HALOS

HALOS

DESIGNER Małgorzata Pawłowska
PHOTOGRAPHER Katarzyna Rutkowska

DESIGNER Marie Pauly
PHOTOGRAPHER Missy Donovan Photography

DESIGNER Victoria Ketcham
PHOTOGRAPHER The Dream Choice

HALOS

DESIGNER Diana Thompson
PHOTOGRAPHER April Walsh Freckled Fox Photography

Coco Chanel

"I don't do fashion. I am fashion."

HALOS

DESIGNER JoAnn Marie Vaught
PHOTOGRAPHER Helen Barker

DESIGNER Jane Goldfinch
PHOTOGRAPHER Sawyers Photography

DESIGNER Courtney Kroymann
PHOTOGRAPHER Beth Joy Photography

Design by **Sue Yamaguchi**
Photography by **Brandon Yamaguchi**

DESIGNER Sue Yamaguchi
PHOTOGRAPHER Brandon Yamaguchi

A beautiful Haku Lei can be created by using the technique of braiding and winding brightly colored flowers and greenery to form a unique traditional Hawaiian headpiece. The Haku Lei can even be worn around the neck or to adorn the brim of a woven hat.

1

Cut flowers and foliage stems approximately 2 to 3 inches in length and place in water.

2

Soak the raffia for 5 to 10 minutes. Measure the diameter of the wearer's head. Braid the soaked raffia the length measured plus 10 inches. For example, if the head measures 22 inches, add 10 inches for a total of 32 inches. Lay the braid spine flat and tie a piece of raffia 5 inches from the start of the braid.

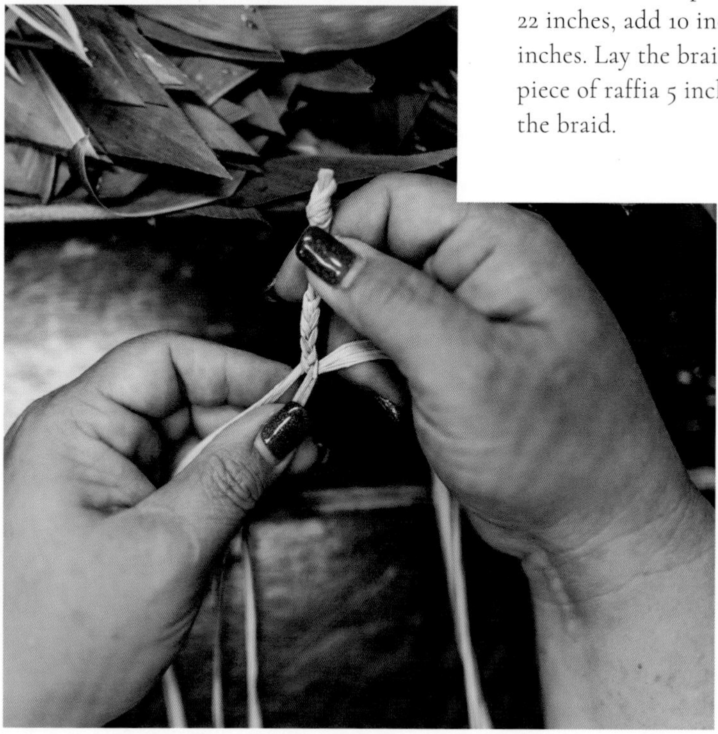

3

Lay a piece of Ti Leaf flat with the spine. Wind the raffia around the Ti Leaf in a circular motion. Firmly pull the raffia to secure.

4

Place a piece of shinobu fern on top of the Ti Leaf and repeat the circular winding technique. Firmly pull the raffia to secure. Repeat with the waxflower. Continue repeating this sequence (Ti Leaf, shinobu fern, waxflower, privet berries, Song of India, *Bougainvillea*, *Cymbidium*, *Mokara* orchids, *Plumeria*, spray roses and *Leucaena leucocephala*) throughout the lei to create the pattern of overlapping layers. The tension between layers must be strong enough to ensure that the botanical materials stay in place without showing the raffia spine.

The key to creating a Haku Lei is to place the flowers and foliage in a consistent width throughout the lei.

When your raffia tie piece becomes too short to continue winding, secure the raffia to the spine by using a half knot. Cut another piece of raffia and tie it where you ended working. Continue winding the raffia around the flowers and foliage.

5

When you have 5 inches remaining at the end of the braid, tie off the raffia with a knot. Sprinkle the Haku lei with water and place in a plastic bag until ready for use.

MATERIALS

Leucaena leucocephala
Bougainvillea
Cymbidiums
Plumeria
Spray roses
Waxflowers
Ti leaf
Song of India
Shinobu fern
Mokara orchids
Privet berries
White lisianthus
Raffia

ACCESSORIES

SHOES

DESIGNER Tobey Nelson
PHOTOGRAPHER Suzanne Rothmeyer Photography

DESIGNER Anika Wilson
PHOTOGRAPHER Kate Mallett Photography

Christian Louboutin

"Shoes transform your body language and attitude. They lift you physically and emotionally."

DESIGNER Carol Jillian
PHOTOGRAPHER Jay Brans

BOAS & CAPES

DESIGNER Natalie Ransom
PHOTOGRAPHER Asia Dore Photography

DESIGNER Julia Rose
PHOTOGRAPHER Ingrid Coles Photography

DESIGNER Julia Rose
PHOTOGRAPHER Cloud Catcher Studios

DESIGNER Courtney Kroymann
PHOTOGRAPHER Beth Joy Photography

Yves Saint Laurent

"Fashions fade, style is eternal."

DESIGNER Tobey Nelson
PHOTOGRAPHER Suzanne Rothmeyer Photography

DESIGNER Jorge Uribe
PHOTOGRAPHER Maurizio Guzman

GARTER BELTS

(Left) **DESIGNER** Robyn Dahlson, **PHOTOGRAPHER** L. Johnhell Media

DESIGNER Valen Ibarra, **PHOTOGRAPHER** Adrian Valazques

STEP-BY-STEP / *Floral Scarf*

Design by **Lea Romanowski**
Photography by **Fly Free Photography**

Add a little pizzazz and attitude to your night out by creating a custom floral scarf to complement your party dress. These flowers to wear will make you feel and look like the "Belle of the Ball."

1

Take measurements of the individual who will be wearing the scarf: Start at the lowest point in of the back, up over the shoulder, around the entire neck, and then down to the desired length in the front. Make a note of the measurement.

2

Add three inches to the above measurement and cut one piece of felt and two pieces of satin ribbon to this length.

3

Hot glue the two pieces of satin ribbon together, side-by-side with a slight overlap.

4

Using the original measurement, add six inches and cut a piece of rustic wire; cover the wire with floral tape.

5

Connect the two ends of the rustic wire with a two-inch overlap. Tape into place. Shape the wire into a long oval flaring the ends out a bit.

6

Lay the shaped wire on top the felt. Mark a dot with a felt pen where the two ends will overlap around the neck. It's important to allow 1-1 ½ inches for give. Hot glue a magnet on each marked dot. Press down to secure.

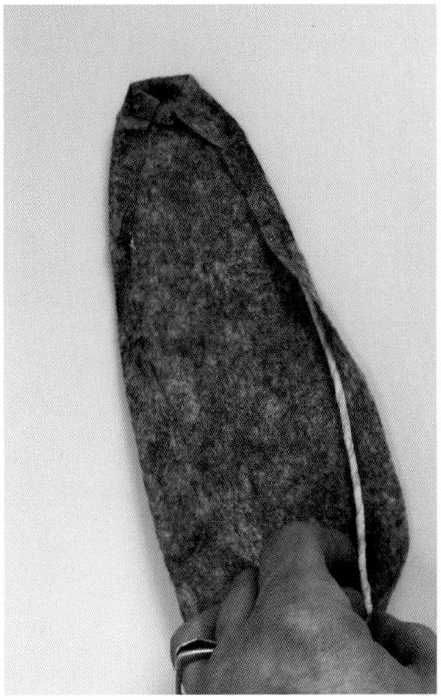

7

Starting in the center and moving outward, fold the felt over the wire and secure with hot glue. It will look like a thin paddle.

BOTANICAL MATERIALS

Ti Leaves

Mini calla

Phalaenopsis orchids

Asparagus fern

Eryngium 'Supernova'

Scabiosa

MATERIALS

No. 40 double satin ribbon

No. 40 felt

Rustic wire

Hot glue gun

Magnet

Floral tape

Floral adhesive

8

Lay the satin piece on the table. Place the felt-wire piece on top of the satin material. Fold the satin over the wire and secure; cut away any extra fabric.

9

It is very important to try on the scarf before attaching botanicals in order to shape the wire into a scarf. It is best to work with a mannequin. The magnets should click together.

10

Cold glue the botanicals to the scarf one variety at a time in a desired pattern; fill in with Asparagus fern. Spray the floral scarf with a finishing spray and place in cooler for 12-24 hours.

MASKS

DESIGNER JoAnn Marie Vaught
PHOTOGRAPHER Helen Barker

COMBS

(Combs, from top)
DESIGNER Claudia Krupple, **PHOTOGRAPHER** Photography by Bambi
DESIGNER Brenda Garcia, **PHOTOGRAPHER** Brenda Garcia

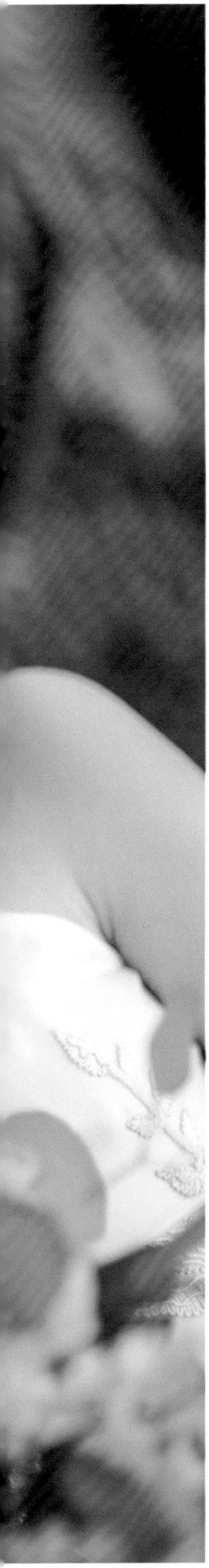

HEADBANDS

(Headbands, from left)
DESIGNER Kelly Robinson, **PHOTOGRAPHER** Krista Fox
DESIGNER JoAnn Marie Vaught, **PHOTOGRAPHER** Helen Barker

STEP-BY-STEP | *Modern Boho Floral Headband*

Design by **Gina Thresher**
Photography by **Rebecca Anne Photography**

Let the little girl inside emerge with a fun and modern Boho floral headband. Create one for a bridal party, a birthday celebration or just because anyone can wear flowers for the day.

1

Cut a piece of gold flat wire to the desired length creating a headband. Form the wire into the shape of a headband curling the ends.

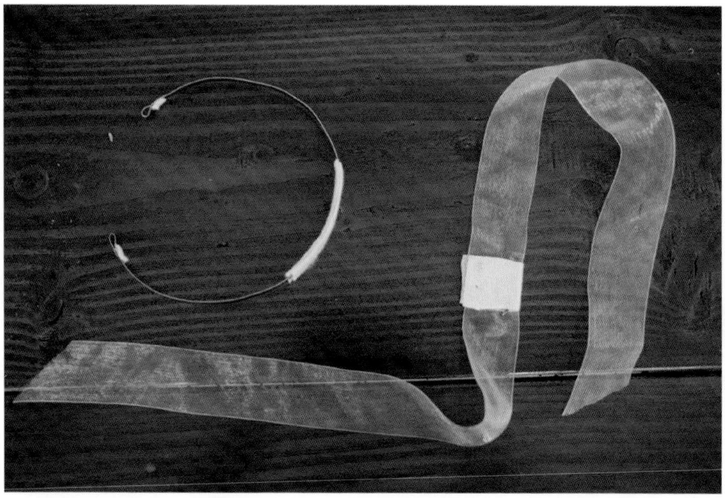

2

Cut your botanical materials stems to the desired lengths.

3

Using floral adhesive, attach the foliage to the felt. To create a voluminous look, layer foliage on top foliage.

4

Glue the dwarf Lily of the Valley. Add another layer by gluing the *Ranunculus* and spray roses on top the dwarf Lily of the Valley.

5

Cold glue the jasmine, waxflowers, Spanish moss and more dwarf Lily of the Valley.

BOTANICAL MATERIALS

Eucalyptus "Silver Dollar"

Dusty Miller

Ranunculus

Dwarf Lily of the Valley shrub

Jasmine

Waxflowers

Spanish moss

Spray rose "Snowflake"

MATERIALS

Gold Flat Wire

Hot glue

Felt

Floral adhesive

Organza sheer No. 3 ribbon

6

Thread the No. 3 organza ribbon through curled ends.

DESIGNER Gina Thresher
PHOTOGRAPHER Rebecca Anne Photography

HEADPIECES

HEAD PIECES

DESIGNER Tobey Nelson
PHOTOGRAPHER Shannon Beauclair, Beauclair Photography

Giambattista Valli

"The hardest thing in fashion is not to be known for a logo, but to be known for a silhouette."

DESIGNER Natalie Ransom
PHOTOGRAPHER Kim Lincoln Photography

DESIGNER Julia Rose, **PHOTOGRAPHER** Hossay

(Left) **DESIGNER** Carol Jillian, **PHOTOGRAPHER** Jay Barns

DESIGNER Tobey Nelson
PHOTOGRAPHER Suzanne Rothmeyer

DESIGNER Jennifer Reed
PHOTOGRAPHER Sarah Collier

DESIGNER Julia Rose
PHOTOGRAPHER Intricate Exposures

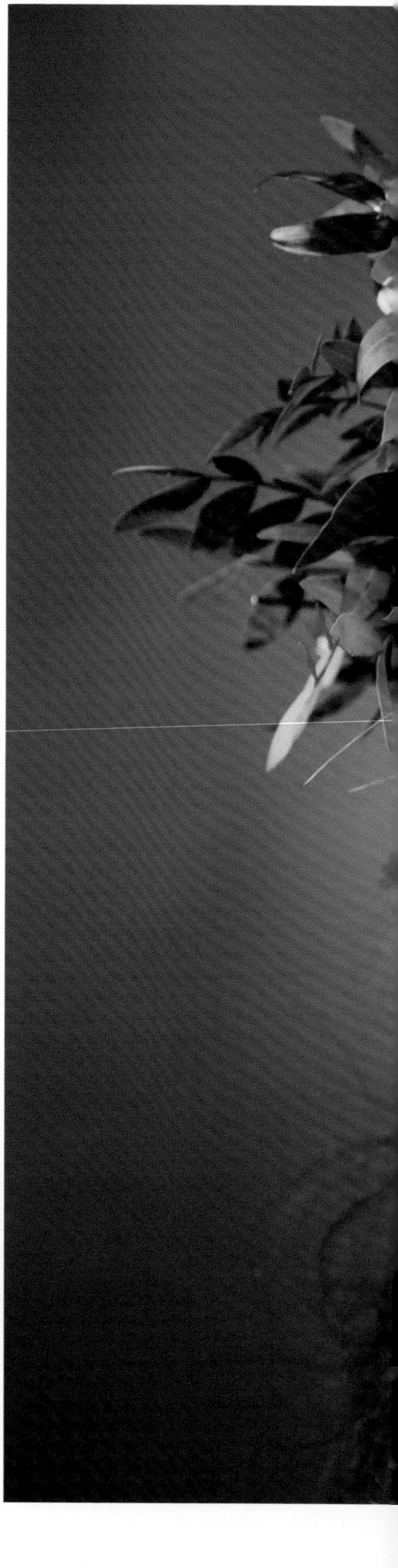

DESIGNER Beata Kaas
PHOTOGRAPHER Kanwal Malnotra , Kanwal Photography

DESIGNER Julia Griffin
PHOTOGRAPHER Holden Photo

Oscar de la Renta

"Fashion is about dressing according to what's fashionable. Style is more about being yourself."

DESIGNER Annise Lorel
PHOTOGRAPHER Tristen Williams

DESIGNER Coral Shortt
PHOTOGRAPHER Peter Bryuns

ABOUT THE DESIGNERS

Ania Norwood AFID, CFD, EMC, CCD
Ania Norwood's Polish heritage and background in civil engineering, architectural design as well as her love of interior design, photography and art have been extremely beneficial in the creation of her floral designs. A floral artist since 2002, she is a freelance designer and owner of **Ania Norwood Designs** in Laguna Beach, California.

Anika Wilson
A farmer-florist, Anika Wilson is a one-woman show specializing in design-driven weddings and events at **Bad Rabbit Flowers** in Westbrook, Maine. "I try to add a light, delicate floral touch to a natural look without it becoming too overpowering."

Annise Lorel
Annise is the owner, creative lead, and principal designer at **Bespoke Blossoms** in Victoria, British Columbia, Canada and has been designing for over nine years. Bespoke Blossoms, which she created with a commitment to environmental sustainability and social consciousness, has won many design awards in the wedding and event industry. At an early age, Annise developed a passion for floral design. While she loves designing bespoke arrangements, she especially enjoys creating couture wearable floral art and feels the fleeting beauty of wearable flowers makes them that much more extraordinary.

Beata Kaas EMC
Combining her architectural background with her passion for flowers, Beata is the owner of a concept design studio **Kaas Floral Design** in Toronto, Ontario, Canada. Beata creates stunning visual floral art pieces by using flowers in an innovative way. "The earth goddess head pieces are modern in expression with touches of light and transparency."

Betsy Mason Borden
Owner of **Dancing Daisies Floral**, a home-based boutique floral studio in Farmington, Utah, Betsy Mason Borden has been in the floral industry since 2014 where she focuses her wearable work on collaboration. "We wanted to create something that is on the verge of being the next high-fashion yet accessible trend."

Brenda Garcia
A Mexican born florist now living in Spain, Brenda Garcia owns **Floral Atelier** in Barcelona. "I love to create magic little worlds with different materials and textures."

Carol Jillian
Owner of **Jillian Design** in The Hills, Texas, Carol Jillian is a botanical couture artist who sees endless possibilities. "I find inspiration from nature, the human form and the desire to combine the two with a seamless flow. This is my passion."

Claudia Kruppel
Claudia Kruppel is a trained florist who is a plant and flower lover. An educator, she owns **Plant Presents** in Gympie, Queensland, Australia where she shares rare and unusual plants with her local customers. "I help a breeding program of endangered air plants."

Coral Shortt
Coral Shortt of **Epanouir Flower Studio** in Cape Town, South Africa, is a retail florist for 13 years, who now focuses exclusively on events and weddings. "I am inspired by mechanics, which drive the creation of a floral wearable that I have been inspired to make. I love floral art and design and am also now teaching floral mechanics and business skills."

Courtney Kroymann AIFD, CFD, CFDA
A floral designer since 2007, Courtney is inspired by nature to create with the beautiful flowers in the Pacific Northwest. Owner of **Designs by Courtney** in Kirkland, Washington, she enjoys playing with different textures and flowers. "With these pieces, I was trying to create an inspired whimsical look with a woodland fairy style for drama."

Debbie Smyl
In the floral industry since 1989, Debbie Smyl has turned an old wood shop into a quaint floral studio. She is the owner of **Westcove Treasures** in St. Paul, Alberta, Canada, and is fascinated with floral couture details and mechanics. She has been dressing up her daughter since birth. Debbie stepped into the floral fashion world when her daughter wanted to create a modeling portfolio.

Denise Kelly
Inspired by the lush Green Springs Garden park in Northern Virginia, Denise Kelly has been a floral designer at **All RelEvents** in Chantilly, Virginia for the past seven years . "I want to include the colors of the flora covering the park gardens."

Diana Thompson
A Latin American soul living a dream, Diana Thompson is the owner of **Samantha's Garden** in Rodgers, Arizona. She is an advocate for healing the heart through creativity. "We are made in this image of our Creator therefore we are made to create! My passion is to share the Love and Grace through the beauty of flowers."

Donald Yim AIFD, CFD, PFCI
With a passion for flowers, a sense of exploration and an eye for beauty, Donald has been in floral design for over 20 years and is currently the creative director of **West Van Florist** in Vancouver, Canada as well as a Floriology Institute education specialist and design director with Smither-Oasis Floral Products. Deeply influenced by the eastern and western cultures, Donald has a unique approach to floral design and aesthetics. "Bamboo is in my culture, so this is why this design starts with the bamboo structure."

Elli Jespersen
The owner of **Small Flowers** in Calgary, Alberta, Canada for the past 20 years, Elli Jespersen grew up spending time in her grandmothers' gardens. "My very first job was in a flowers shop and I have never looked back. I love flowers and fashion and find nothing quite as satisfying as being able to combine two of my passions together."

Françoise Weeks
Françoise Weeks, born in Belgium, has infused her work with a quintessential European reverence for flowers and nature. Combined with creativity and mechanical ingenuity, she has crystalized her singular style of textural woodlands and botanical haute couture pieces, garnering a global following. As an international educator, her generosity of knowledge and perspective in use of floral materials, structure and techniques, create rigorous and exciting learning opportunities for her students to explore all that nature has to offer. Françoise's studio, **Françoise Weeks Florist**, is located in Portland, Oregon where she also teaches and offers online courses as well. Her dynamic work has been published in national and international publications.

Gina Threscher AIFD, CFD, EMC
Owner of **From the Ground Up Floral**, an event and wedding studio in Kent, Washington, Gina Threscher is passionate about teaching floral design, producing podcasts and creating. Gina's inspiration behind her floral couture creations come from something as simple as a floret of a flower or a lipstick color.

Jane Goldfinch
Jane Goldfinch is the owner of **Couture Botanical**, a floral design studio based in the beautiful Hunter Valley of New South Wales, Australia. Her designs range from modern to romantic to lush garden-inspired unstructured bouquets. She specializes in unique flower crowns that are big, bold and a little avantgarde.

Jennifer Reed
For over 16 years, Jennifer Reed, owner of **Jennifer Designs** in Mullica Hills, New Jersey, has created unique floral designs for a variety of events. Jennifer believes that floral design, as well as all forms of art, should make you "feel" and be fun. "My design philosophy is to incorporate my love of all mediums of art and translate them into floral form. I draw my inspiration from my extensive experience in the arts to create pieces that emphasize sculptural composition, focus on items found in nature and evoke feeling with color. It's important to pay attention to the little design details."

JoAnn Marie Vaught
JoAnn Marie Vaught, owner of **JM Designs**, Bentonville, Arkansas, uses her extensive knowledge of floral design, combined with her training in sculpture design. to create unique floral couture deigns that are fully functional and beautiful. An artist with 15 years of experience using botanicals as a medium, JoAnn opened her own event design firm in 2017.

Jorge Uribe AIFD, CFD, EMC
Jorge Uribe, owner and creative floral artist of **Urban Floral LLC** in Wolcott, Connecticut, shares his floral creativity through the lens of his camera and his passion for photography. With his ability to capture unique moments in pictures, he allows us to step into time now frozen forever and experience his creative world. His insatiable curiosity, willingness to always be a student of floristry and his experimentation with combining and manipulating different elements has been the key to his creative art for the past 15 years.

Julia Griffin
A flower farmer and floral designer in Detroit, Michigan, Julia Griffin is owner of **Willa Rose Floral**. Julia grows all types of unusual flowers for her design work. "I love creating non-traditional and unexpected pieces with flowers. My design style is whimsical,
natural and free flowing."

Julia Marie Schmitt AIFD, CFD, EMC, ICPF, PFCI
An international floral artist, presenter and educator, Julia began her floral career in 2008 when she started designing at her mother's "retirement hobby flower shop". It did not take long for flowers to become her passion and her life. She travels the global sharing her passion with designers as well as conducts floral art workshops for all educational levels at her floral studio and flower shop Flowers by Julia Marie in rural Marceline, Missouri.

ABOUT THE DESIGNERS

Julia Rose
Botanical artist and owner of **Flowers by Julia Rose** in Brisbane, Queensland, Australia, she designs floral culture for the "imagery" and "creating for the sake of creating". With over 20 years experience in the floral industry, Julia Rose is a floral educator who is now recognized for her organic and naturally eclectic designs. "Everything you do shapes you in a certain way. All my failures have made me stronger. For artists, do what you love, and people will see that; your passion will shine through."

Kelly Robinson
Kelly Robinson is the owner and creative director of **Ooh La Design** in Fonthill, Ontario, Canada; she has been designing for 10 years. Kelly enjoys creating floral couture for editorial photo shots in the Niagara Wine Country.

Kiki Uyede
Relatively new to the floral industry, Kiki Uyede, owner of **Hanaki Floral Design** in Vancouver, British Columbia, Canada, is influenced by *Ikebana*. Her free form style is versatile. "I create floral headbands that can be styled to be worn as a choker. I also created lush bouquets to go with the headbands."

Kristen Janes
A 23-year-veteran of the floral industry, Kristen Janes owns **Kio Kreations** in Plainfield, Illinois. Having earned a BFA in illustration, she tries to work art and creative ideas into everything she designs. "I love making floral necklaces that feel like real jewelry. I use leather and clasps and other jewelry making materials as part of my mechanics and then use interesting blooms and textures to create wearable floral art."

Laura Draghici
Owner of **Chic Fleuriste** in Ploiseti, Romania, Laura Draghici entered the floral industry after taking a floral class and dabbling in creating arrangements for friends. A successful bank manager with an EMBA (Executive Master of Business Administration) and years of financial experience, Laura followed her heart, changed careers and now is a successful flower shop owner. "It is important to follow your dreams. If you work and think you can do it, you can reach your dreams."

Lea Romanowski AIFD, CFD, CAFA, CAFD
A floral jack-of-all-trades, floral artist and educator, Lea Romanowski, owner of **Designing on the Edge**, in Calgary, Alta, Canada is a 37- year veteran of the floral industry. With her unique approach to design, her artistic expressions are always a surprise in creativity. With her mind-set of "if you can conceive it, you can achieve it," she continues to blur the lines and create floral jewelry that is always unexpected and spectacular.

Loann Burke AIFD, AAF, CFD, PFCI
An event specialist for over 20 years at **Furst Florist** in Dayton, Ohio, Loann Burke shares her expertise and time with Smither-Oasis as a design director. "This dress was a complete labor of love for my only daughter. She has three older brothers, so this was my first opportunity to do something like this for my child. It was created for her senior photos."

Małgorzata Pawłowska
As the owner of **Dzikie Pole Małgorzata Pawłowska** in Kozłów Biskupi, Poland, Malgorzata is a Master florist and floral fundamental ambassador who has a love of flowers, craft and fantasy. "It is from all these passions that my floral creations are born."

Marie Pauly
Specializing in weddings and events for 30 years, Marie Pauly is the owner of **Wild Orchid Custom Floral Design** in Maple Park, Illinois. Marie loves to step outside the box and try new creative floral designs. She enjoys collaborating with local businesses as she mixes on-trend styles with a romantic twist.

Natalie Ranson
Owner of **Pozie by Natalie** in Bellingham, Washington, Natalie started working in the floral industry in Bellingham before branching out on her own as Pozie by Natalie in 2015. "Because my work is also my joy, I make sure that my floral art is fresh and extraordinary. Whether it's living jewelry, a bouquet, a centerpiece, arbor, or crown, I pour my imagination and inspiration into every striking creation for weddings, special occasions, business and charity events."

Orit Hertz EMC
After leaving a career in hi-tech, Orit Hertz, an event and freelance designer from Israel, has been bringing together the world of fashion design and fresh flowers in various floral productions since 2012. "Flowers have always been my great love. I love the beauty, the colors, the vitality, the joy they always seem to create and their wonderful scents."

Robyn Dahlson
Growing up in the floral industry, Robyn Dahlson began her career first on a flower farm, then worked for a wholesaler. "Floristry has become a huge creative outlet and it is an honor to use gifts from Mother Nature to design." With family being the center of her life, Robyn has dedicated her work to memory of her grandmother, the Matriarch of **Mayesh Wholesale**, her family's business.

Rupali Shete Sadalage AIFD, CFD
Originally from India, a science graduate who wanted to become a doctor, Rupali Shete Sadalage channeled her energies into interior design. Realizing her passion for creativity, she eventually became a floral designer. She is a freelance designer and owner of **Rupali Shete** in the Chicago, Illinois Area.

Sue Yamaguchi AIFD, CFD, EMC
Owner of **Su-V Expressions** in Honolulu, Hawaii, Sue Yamaguchi has been in the floral industry since 1993. Specializing in weddings and events, Sue's passion for flowers and her incredible ability to create structures of any occasion sparks her desire to continue to explore what the floral world has to offer.

Susanne Law AIFD, CFD, EMC
An educator and floral artist for over 20 years, Susanne is the head designer at **La Belle Fleur Floral Boutique** in Surrey, British Columbia, Canada. She enjoys challenging herself with new pursuits such as competitions and creative design projects. "I love creating floral couture because it's an opportunity to showcase flowers, foliage and plant materials in an intriguing way. The value and uniqueness of each floral material is magnified when it is used for its color and texture, especially in a smaller scale of work."

Tobey Nelson
Landscape horticultural designer turned event and wedding floral designer Tobey Nelson, owner of **Tobey Nelson Events and Designs** in Langley, Washington, incorporates the techniques and mechanics she learned for corsage and bridal work into her passion for floral couture. "I just like it. The thing that draws me to plants is the plant energy. Why not celebrate the beauty of people and especially women by putting flowers on them?"

Tuba Belgin Oskan EMC
Based in Istanbul, Turkey, floral designer Tuba Belgin Oskan has been creating floral wonders in her studio, **Natura Karma**, since 2014. Originally an expert in destination and event management, Tuba discovered her creative side in the years after her beloved mother passed away and she was in search of a more emotionally satisfactory career path. Creating with flowers has allowed Tuba to form a spiritual connection with her late mother and to take joy in sharing her unique designs and floral arrangements with her friends, family and clientele.

Valen Ibarra
Owner of **Blumenhaus** in Denver, Colorado, Valen Ibarra has created a floral company that focuses on her creativity and representing herself as an artist. "BlumenHaus is somewhere where the only limit is yourself. I enjoy thinking of unique designs. I love bringing my visions to life. I love when things turn out exactly how I saw it, or better."

Wendy Evans
Co-owner of **Details Dallas Floral** in Flower Mound, Texas, Wendy Evans met her business partner Rochelle marching in the drum corps. "Our passion is creating a fun and unique floral experience for each customer. We both put a piece of ourselves in our work and send that love through the flowers. I am especially inspired by the deconstruction of each bloom to create a repetitive pattern."

Victoria Ketcham
Owner of Studio based **Upton Grey Floral** in Pasadena, California, Victoria Ketcham celebrates exquisitely natural, abundant designs with an emphasis on seasonal and American blooms. "I believe that the most beautiful floral designs 'leave space for the butterflies', as Mother Nature intended. As such, you'll often find flowering branches and elegant line flowers reaching out of arrangements, inviting the eyes to wander and discover gorgeous fragrant blooms tucked within the design – not unlike the discovery of walking through a garden."

Giorgio Armani

“Elegance is not standing out, but being remembered.”